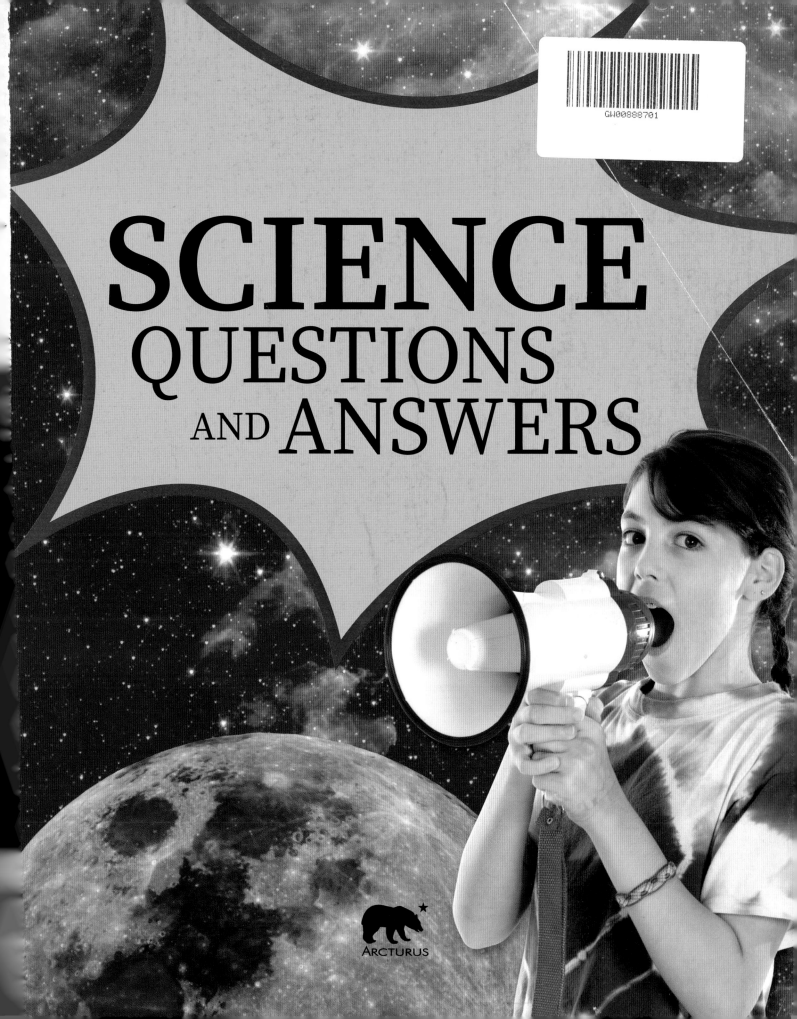

SCIENCE
QUESTIONS
AND ANSWERS

ARCTURUS

This edition published in 2020 by Arcturus Publishing Limited
26/27 Bickels Yard, 151–153 Bermondsey Street,
London SE1 3HA

Copyright © Arcturus Holdings Limited

All rights reserved. No part of this publication may be reproduced,
stored in a retrieval system, or transmitted, in any form or by any means,
electronic, mechanical, photocopying, recording or otherwise, without
prior written permission in accordance with the provisions of the
Copyright Act 1956 (as amended). Any person or persons who do any
unauthorised act in relation to this publication may be liable to criminal
prosecution and civil claims for damages.

Edited by Joe Harris and Samantha Noonan
Designed by Ian Winton
Cover Design: Steve Flight

ISBN: 978-1-83940-278-4
CH003577NT
Supplier: 29, Date 0320, Print run 10013

Printed in China

What is STEM?

STEM is a world-wide initiative that
aims to cultivate an interest in
Science, Technology, Engineering,
and Mathematics, in an effort
to promote these disciplines to
as wide a variety of students as
possible.

Picture credits: All images supplied by Shutterstock, except for the following:
Corbis: p90 b (Bennett Dean/ Eye Ubiquitous/ Corbis), p102 t (Xinhua Press/ Corbis). FLPA: p54 t, p55 t,
p58, t. NASA: p110 bl, p118 bl, p120 c, p120 b. Sally Henry and Trevor Cook: p86 b.

Contents

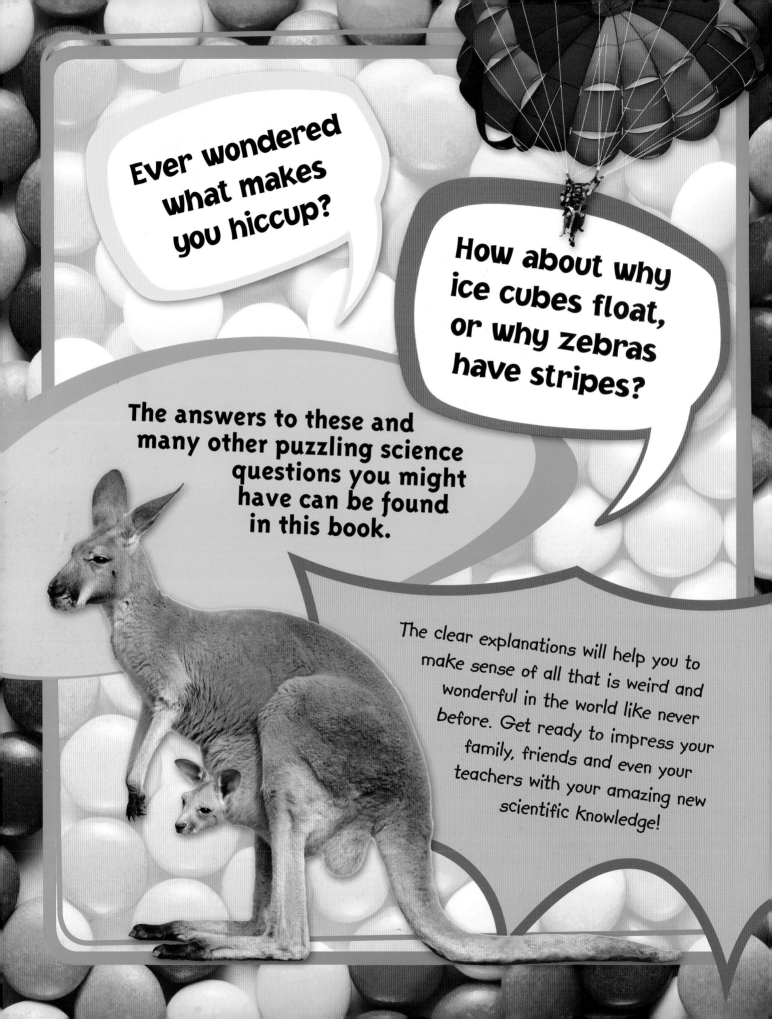

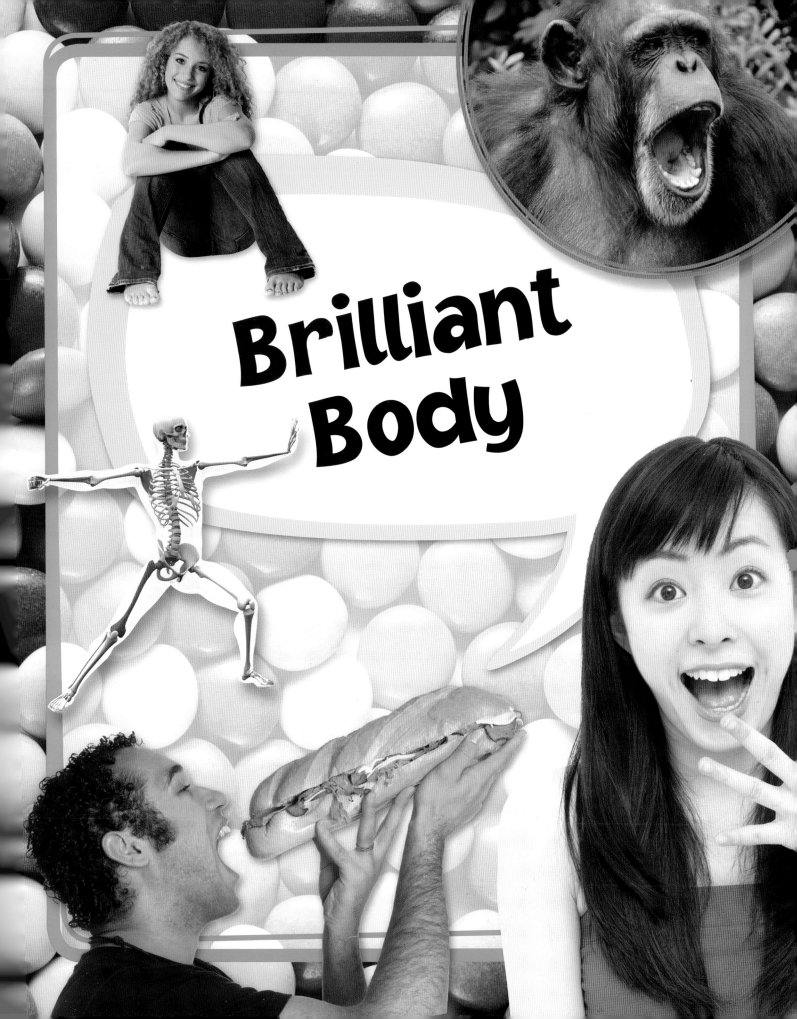

Brilliant Body

It's break time

It's time to bone up on those parts of you that sticks and stones can break. But how much do you really know about the job that your skeleton does?

Why don't you laugh when you hit your funny bone?

Because it hurts! And it hurts so much because you've just hit a nerve. Most nerves are protected by bone or muscle. But the ulnar nerve in your elbow is the largest unprotected nerve in your body. It's possible that the term "funny bone" comes from the name of a nearby bone in your upper arm, the humerus.

Do you grow more bones as you get older?

No, you do just the opposite. Babies are born with more than 300 bones. Adults have 206 bones. The number goes down because bones join together to become bigger, stronger bones. And that starts to happen when you're about 12 years old.

Why do bones show up more clearly than other parts of the body in X-rays?

That's because X-rays are a form of radiation, just like light. The calcium in your bones absorbs X-rays. But the same X-rays mostly pass through softer cells in your body because they are mostly made up of water. It's like shining a light in the fog. You see a car or a tree, but the light passes through the fog itself.

What is the largest bone in the body?

The femur, or thigh bone, is the largest bone in the body. It is also the strongest. The femur is in the upper leg and connects the pelvis to the knee. It needs to be big and strong because it supports the whole body. An average adult femur is about 45 cm (18 inches) long. That's nearly 200 times longer than the stirrup – the smallest bone in body, found in the ear.

I beg your pardon

Achoo! You know you should say "excuse me" when you've made people turn around and look at you... Now it's time to learn the reasons for what just happened!

HIC!

What makes you hiccup?

It's pretty easy to say what makes you hiccup. Usually, you hiccup because something has irritated your stomach. And we know what a hiccup is. It's a sudden tightening of your breathing muscles. The "hic" sounds when a piece of skin flaps shut over your windpipe. The real mystery is the purpose of hiccups. Scientists still can't agree on that one.

Is yawning catching?

Yes, it is, but no one is quite sure why. Human beings and chimpanzees are the only animals that yawn when they see each other yawn. But it gets even stranger. Very small children don't yawn when someone near them does. As they get older, people seem to learn to do copycat yawning. So a single yawn can set a whole roomful of people off!

How fast is the air in a sneeze?

Air rushes out of your nose and mouth at more than 100 miles per hour (160 km/h) when you sneeze. It's one of your body's ways of keeping your nose clear. Usually, you have no control over whether you're going to sneeze. That's because it is a natural reflex and not something you can plan. A typical sneeze contains up to 40,000 tiny drops of liquid mixed in with the air.

How loud is the loudest burp?

A burp is a harmless way of getting rid of air or gas that you might have swallowed. Carbonated drinks often make you burp because they are full of gas. Normally, you can control how the gas will be released, so you can keep things pretty quiet. The world record for the loudest burp is 107 decibels. That's as loud as a lawn mower running next to you.

9

Act your age

Growing up is a one-way street, and there's no going backward! Of course, all the interesting stuff happens in between birth and death, so let's find out a little more about what happens as you get older.

How do our bodies know when to stop growing?

Our bodies are programmed to stop growing because of messages in our genes. Young children have "growth plates" at the ends of their long bones. These plates are made of soft material that grows. When children reach their late teens, their genes send out signals. These signals tell the body to make substances that seal the growth plates. This stops the bones from growing any more.

Do people's nails grow even after they have died?

No, they don't. But it might seem as though nails (and hair) grow because we interpret what we see incorrectly. In life, our flesh contains lots of water. When people die, their skin dries out and shrinks. As the soft parts lose water and shrivel, the hard parts stay the same length. So it looks as though they've grown. Creepy, huh?

Why can't boys grow beards?

Your body uses chemicals called hormones to carry messages. A hormone called testosterone tells a man's face to grow hair. When a boy's body begins to change at puberty, his body starts to produce testosterone. This hormone leads to other changes, such as a deeper voice and more muscles. Women and girls, like young boys, don't have the testosterone to create these changes.

Why do people live longer than they did in the past?

People in Ancient Rome had an average life span of just 28 years. These days, the average world life expectancy has risen to 67 years, and in the United States, most people can expect to live to about 78. This is because we now have better food and medicine to fight disease. Also, people know how important it is to stay clean in order to stop the spread of germs.

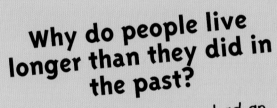

11

Just be sensible

Your body uses all of its senses to "make sense" of the world around you. How much sense do you think you can make from these questions?

Why can't you tickle yourself?

Scientists think that you laugh when you're tickled because you're a little bit scared. It's a way of letting off steam. The feeling of being tickled is like when a small insect crawls over you. You want to wriggle and maybe scream because you don't know what might happen. Similarly, your body is a little worried when someone surprises you with a tickle. But you can't surprise yourself – so you can't tickle yourself.

Why don't you taste things when you have a cold?

It's because two of your senses – taste and smell – are so closely linked. Although you may think you just taste food when you're eating, it's really a combination of both taste and smell. Your nose gets blocked when you have a cold, so you don't smell things well. If you can't smell what you're eating, it's harder to get the full taste of it.

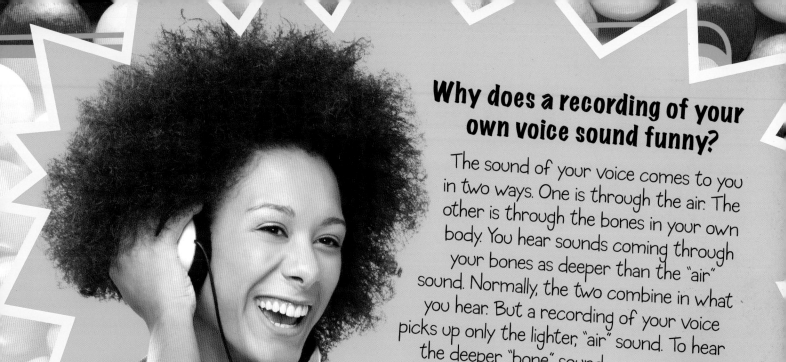

Why does a recording of your own voice sound funny?

The sound of your voice comes to you in two ways. One is through the air. The other is through the bones in your own body. You hear sounds coming through your bones as deeper than the "air" sound. Normally, the two combine in what you hear. But a recording of your voice picks up only the lighter, "air" sound. To hear the deeper "bone" sound, try speaking while wearing earplugs.

Why does pepper make you sneeze?

Your nose is designed to let only air pass through. It has three ways to stop other things getting in – small hairs in the nostrils, mucus... and sneezing. These methods either trap invaders or push them out. Dust and other tiny objects tickle the nerves in your nose and make you sneeze. But pepper contains a chemical that makes your nose nerves even more sensitive. So it has a greater chance of making you sneeze.

13

Pick up the pace

Being healthy is all about (pant, pant) being fit and knowing about (puff, puff) how your body works. Once you know a little more about yourself, then you can pick up the pace and get even fitter.

Is there a limit to how fast athletes can run?

Top athletes today are much faster than runners of 100 or even 30 years ago. That's largely because of better food and improved training. There's probably a limit to how fast even the best athlete can go – but we still have many things to find out about what happens in the legs and feet when an athlete runs.

Why is it hard to walk uphill?

Simple, really – it's all because of gravity. That's the force that draws everything toward the core of the Earth. Gravity helps if you're walking or riding your bike downhill because it's pulling in the right direction. Going uphill, though, means working against the same force.

Does your weight vary during the day?

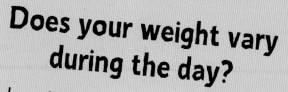

Most people weigh less first thing in the morning than at other times of day. It's mainly because of water. At night, you lose a lot of water as you breathe out and sweat. Then you go to the bathroom when you wake up. Getting rid of all of this water means you lose a bit of weight. During the day, you drink and your weight goes back up again.

60

450

25

Why do some people count calories?

People gain or lose weight because of energy. Food energy is measured in calories. You gain calories when you eat. Exercise and normal body activities burn up energy. That energy is also measured in calories. So people count calories to make sure they eat enough, but not too many calories.

300

15

Pass it on

How many times have you heard that you've got your dad's eyes or your grandma's curly hair? How do we end up being tall, or sporty, or left-handed?

Why are some people left-handed?

Whether you are left- or right-handed is partly controlled by your genes. It's also linked to human development over thousands of years. Scientists believe that being right-handed helped early humans build many skills, such as writing. But left-handed people still had some advantages in fighting and hunting.

Which part of the world has the tallest people?

The tallest humans are among the groups of people living by the River Nile in East Africa. It is common to see men almost 6 foot 8 inches (2 m) tall. If you have tall parents, you are likely to be tall, too – although what you eat and your lifestyle are also important.

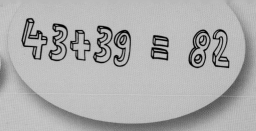

$$43 + 39 = 82$$

Can we inherit the ability to speak French or do difficult calculations?

No one is born with the ability to speak a foreign language or to figure out difficult equations. But people can inherit talents that make it easier for them to learn those skills. It's the same with sports. No one is born a football player or tennis star. But some people find it easier to become good at these sports.

What is a test-tube baby?

Babies develop after a father's sperm cell joins with a mother's egg cell. Normally, that happens in a tube inside the mother's body. Sometimes the tube is damaged and the sperm can't reach the egg. So scientists remove sperm cells and eggs to join them together in a test tube. The new unborn baby (the embryo) is put back inside the mother's womb to develop normally.

Food for thought

They say that some people live to eat and others eat to live. Which of those describes you? Think about it! In the meantime, here are some questions to chew over.

Why does your stomach **rumble** when you're hungry?

Swallowed food passes through the stomach and into the intestines. Muscles squeeze and push the food along as it gets digested. But about two hours after your stomach's emptied, the brain sends a signal to start the squeezing and pushing again. You're probably hungry by that time. But the squeezing and pushing of those muscles around an empty stomach makes quite a noise.

RUMBLE RUMBLE

Does eating fish make you clever?

This advice seemed like a fairy tale for many years. Now scientists believe it is true. People who eat some types of fish (such as tuna and mackerel) do score better on tests. These fish contain a fatty acid called omega-3 that helps more blood flow to your brain.

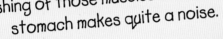

What happens if you swallow a coin?

Luckily, it's usually harmless. Your digestive system is stretchy, so a coin can squeeze through without getting stuck. Plus it covers strange objects with mucus (which is like snot) to help them slide through. The worst thing about swallowing a coin is having to check your poop to make sure you've finally got rid of it!

How does your body know when you're full?

Fat cells in your body send a substance called leptin to your brain. The leptin tells your brain that you don't need more "fuel" to keep your body running, so you should stop eating. Sometimes people produce too much leptin because they have so many fat cells! Too much leptin can confuse the brain and hide the message to stop eating.

Sleep secrets

What happens when you're asleep? Do you dream, talk, or even go for a walk? And how much sleep do you need? Keep reading to discover the secrets of sleep.

Why do children have to go to bed before grown-ups?

Children need to go to bed earlier and get more sleep than adults for two reasons. One is to help the body build up its energy. Growing uses up lots of energy. The other is that sleep itself helps the brain. Scientists believe that a child's brain needs sleep to develop.

Why do we dream?

We all dream, even if we can't remember our dreams in the morning. But doctors can't agree why we dream. Some say that dreams have no real purpose. Others believe that they are a way of dealing with problems that trouble us when we're awake.

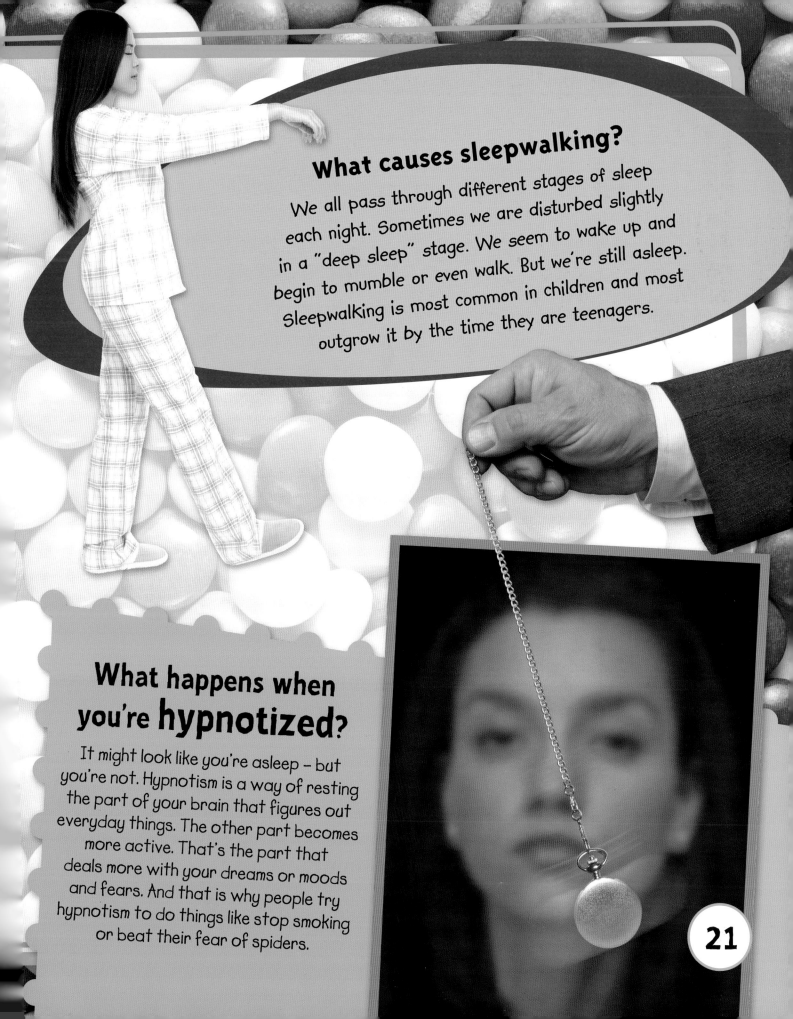

What causes sleepwalking?

We all pass through different stages of sleep each night. Sometimes we are disturbed slightly in a "deep sleep" stage. We seem to wake up and begin to mumble or even walk. But we're still asleep. Sleepwalking is most common in children and most outgrow it by the time they are teenagers.

What happens when you're **hypnotized?**

It might look like you're asleep – but you're not. Hypnotism is a way of resting the part of your brain that figures out everyday things. The other part becomes more active. That's the part that deals more with your dreams or moods and fears. And that is why people try hypnotism to do things like stop smoking or beat their fear of spiders.

Hair, there, and everywhere

Do you spend ages thinking about your hair, or is it something that you're happy to cover with a hat? How would you look with a beard past your feet or if you were bald?

How long could a beard grow?

A man's beard grows about 13 cm (5 in) a year. There's nothing to stop this growth unless he chooses to trim it. The man with the longest beard ever recorded was Hans Langseth of Norway. His beard was 5.65 m (18 ft 6 in) long when he died.

Why do some people have curly hair?

You inherit your type of hair from your parents or grandparents. The way your hair grows depends on the tubes on your head where it starts off. These are called follicles. Hair coming out of a circular follicle grows straight. An oval-shaped follicle sets hair growing in curls.

Why do we have eyebrows?

Scientists believe that eyebrows developed to keep water and sweat from flowing into the eyes. It wouldn't be good to be wiping water away from your eyes if a wolf were chasing you. But eyebrows have another job, too. They send signals to other people about how you're feeling – happy, sad, cross, or surprised.

Why do some men go bald but others don't?

It depends mainly on whether the men on either their mother's or father's side of the family were bald. The gene for baldness destroys the cells that produce hair. Poor diet and sickness can also lead to baldness.

I don't feel good

When your body is under attack from germs and infections, it has lots of ways of fighting back. Sometimes, though, it needs a little help from modern medicine to fight off a disease...

Why do you "run a temperature" when you are sick?

Your body gets warmer when it is fighting an infection. This warming up is called a fever. When it detects an infection, your body produces chemicals called pyrogens. The blood takes the pyrogens to the brain. The brain then "turns up the heat" in order to kill off the germs that are causing the infection.

Why does your nose run in cold weather?

Your nose checks on the air heading down to your lungs. It usually produces mucus to push dust and other particles out of your air passages. Tiny blood vessels in your nostrils become wider in cold weather to warm the air. But the extra blood also makes the nose pump out more mucus, giving you a runny nose.

Why do people get seasick?

Your brain receives signals from other parts of the body. They tell the brain whether you're moving or not. The signal for balance comes from inside your ear. On a rough sea, it tells your brain that you're going up and down. But your eyes see that the tables and walls on the ship aren't moving. Your brain gets confused, and the result is that awful feeling of seasickness.

What was the Black Death?

It was a disease that doctors now call the bubonic plague. Between 1348 and 1350, it swept across Asia and Europe. Millions of people died, including up to half of all Europeans. The disease was spread by fleas. Victims got horrible blisters that turned black. Modern medicine can treat the disease, but people in the Middle Ages usually died if they got it.

Anybody's guess

You've got a lifetime ahead of you to learn more about the marvels of the human body. Here are a few intriguing questions to get you started.

Why do you have a belly button?

You developed inside your mother before you were born. For nine months, you got all the food and oxygen you needed through a tube that went into your stomach. But once you were born, you could use your mouth and nose to eat and breathe. So the doctor tied a knot in the tube and snipped it. This knot is your belly button.

Does poison always taste bad?

No. Sometimes poisonous things can taste good. People sometimes eat mushrooms and then find out that they're poisonous. And some things that smell or taste bad are really good for you. You should always be sure of what you eat.

Home sweet globe

Do you have a globe in your bedroom or classroom? Take a good look at it. Can you imagine being an astronaut, watching the real Earth floating in space? It's an amazing thought, isn't it!

Why does it get hotter in the summer?

During summer, the northern hemisphere (the Earth's top half) is tilted toward the Sun. It gets more sunlight and becomes hotter. At this time, the southern hemisphere has winter. Then things swap six months later when the bottom half is closer to the Sun.

Why is most of the world's land north of the equator?

It just happens to be that way at the moment. Believe it or not, the Earth's continents are slowly moving. Around 300 million years ago, our planet had one big mass of land called Pangaea. It was mainly south of the equator. In another 200 million years, things will probably look different again.

How much of the Earth is covered by ice?

Just under 10 %. Most of that ice is in the glaciers and ice caps of Greenland and Antarctica. Snow and ice also cover mountains in other parts of the world all year long.

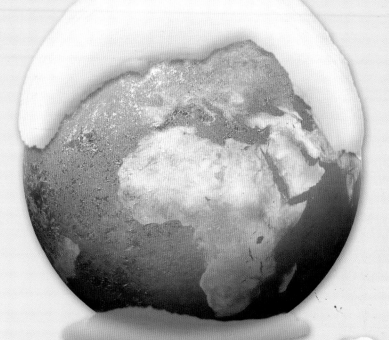

How far away is the horizon?

It depends on your height! The taller, or higher up you are, the greater the distance you'll be able to see before the curve of the Earth dips out of sight. For a girl who is 4 foot 7 inches (1.4 m) tall, the horizon would be 2.6 miles (4.2 km) away. But if she stood on a 10 foot (3 m) ladder, the horizon would be 4.6 miles (7.5 km) away.

HORIZON >

29

Stormy weather

Help! Frogs are bouncing off my umbrella! Straws are flying by like spears, and my ears are ringing from all that thunder! And I thought the weather forecast said "a slight chance of a shower."

Does it really rain frogs?

Yes, but not very often. A very powerful storm can suck frogs and fish up from rivers, lakes, and the sea. They are held up by strong, spinning winds. Then they fall back down when the winds weaken.

Can the wind really drive a straw through a telegraph pole?

Yes, it can, if the wind is strong enough. Tornado winds blow at more than 300 miles per hour (500 km/h), making harmless objects into deadly weapons. But isn't a straw too weak? Not if one end is blocked. Then the air rushes in and pushes out on the sides. The straw gets stronger, just like a pumped-up bike wheel.

Is the saying "Red sky at night, sailors' delight" really accurate?

Yes, it often is. Rain clouds usually travel from west to east. They look red when the Sun is low. A "red sky at night" means that the Sun's rays are shining on clouds that have already passed to the east. This means that it is less likely to be stormy the next day.

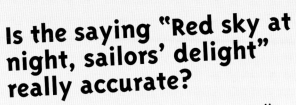

Does every thunderstorm have lightning?

The answer is very simple — yes. Lightning causes thunder. A lightning bolt quickly heats up air. The hot air expands and then quickly cools and contracts. That superfast heating and cooling makes the sound of thunder.

Around and around

Our home, the Earth, is whizzing through space, spinning around twice as fast as a plane flies. Does that make you feel dizzy? You might want to shout, "Stop the world, I want to get off!"

Why don't people in the southern hemisphere fall off?

People in the southern hemisphere are not upside down. It's just that most maps are drawn with the southern hemisphere at the bottom. An upside-down map would be just as accurate. In fact, gravity pulls everything into the core of the Earth, so we all stay on it!

Why don't we feel the Earth spinning?

The Earth rotates (spins) completely around once every 24 hours. That means that it's spinning at 1,070 miles per hour (1,670 km/h). However, we don't feel that motion because we're also moving at the same speed. It's like flying in a plane – you don't feel like you're moving fast.

Is the Earth slowing down?

Yes, it is. The exact length of a day (one complete spin of the planet) on Earth is 23 hours and 56 minutes. However, the Earth is slowing down by about one second every ten years. So in 2,400 years, a day really will last exactly 24 hours.

STOP

Is the Earth completely round?

Not quite! Its spinning makes the Earth a little wider along the equator and shorter at the poles. The distance through the Earth from North Pole to South Pole is less than the distance through the Earth at the equator.

33

The right impression

We can definitely trust our eyes and ears, can't we, when it comes to the world around us? Well, not always! It's time for us to investigate weird happenings such as echoes and mirages.

What is an echo?

An echo is simply a reflection of sound just as a mirror image is a reflection of light. Sound travels in waves. When these waves hit a hard surface, they bounce back. We hear the sound again a little later (once it has gone to the hard surface and back).

Why does the Moon seem so big when it's just rising over the horizon?

Scientists know that it's a trick that our eyes play on us. However, they can't agree on how it works. To show that the Moon doesn't change size, hold a coin out so it just covers the Moon on the horizon. Hold it at the same distance when the Moon is overhead. You won't see any change in size.

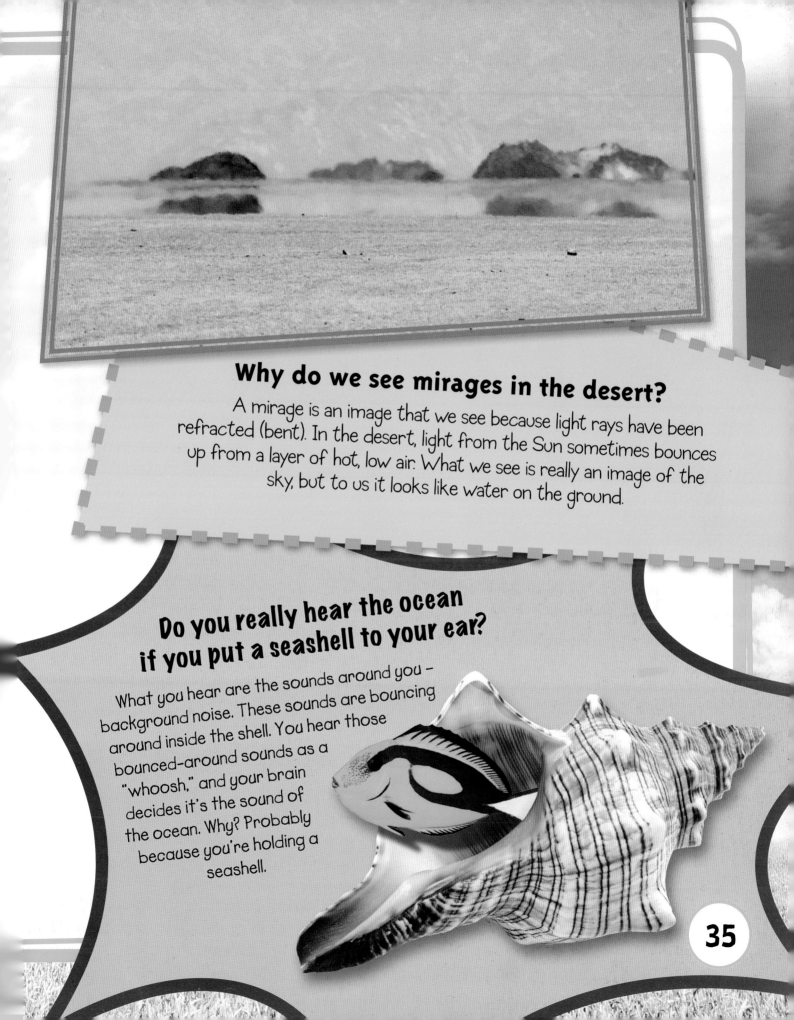

Why do we see mirages in the desert?

A mirage is an image that we see because light rays have been refracted (bent). In the desert, light from the Sun sometimes bounces up from a layer of hot, low air. What we see is really an image of the sky, but to us it looks like water on the ground.

Do you really hear the ocean if you put a seashell to your ear?

What you hear are the sounds around you – background noise. These sounds are bouncing around inside the shell. You hear those bounced-around sounds as a "whoosh," and your brain decides it's the sound of the ocean. Why? Probably because you're holding a seashell.

A large shake, please

The Earth beneath your feet may seem solid and steady. However, our planet's surface is in constant movement. Sometimes that movement results in earthquakes and volcanoes.

Can animals predict earthquakes?

The answer seems to be "yes" for some animals. Frogs and toads can sense slight chemical changes in the water in ponds or lakes. Scientists have noticed similar changes in rocks in the days leading up to earthquakes. Witnesses have seen groups of toads leaving ponds just before earthquakes.

Why do volcanoes erupt?

The Earth's crust (outer layer) is made up of large pieces called plates. Magma, a gooey substance made up of gas and melted rock, lies under the plates. When two plates collide, they may force magma to the surface in a volcanic eruption. The magma that comes out is called lava.

Why do South America and Africa look like pieces of a jigsaw puzzle?

All of the continents were once part of one large landmass. However, the Earth's crust is constantly moving. This movement broke up the giant landmass millions of years ago. The edges of some continents show us where the continents were once joined.

Africa

South America

Could flowing lava really overtake a car?

The speed of a lava flow differs from volcano to volcano. A lot depends on how steep the slope is. The amount of gas mixed in with the molten (melted) rock also affects how "runny" the lava is. Witnesses have recorded lava flowing faster than 38 miles per hour (60 km/h) – fast enough to overtake a car.

Just give me some time

We are used to thinking about time in hours and days, but when it comes to Earth science, things happen much more slooooowly. Much of what we see around us has changed over a long time... and is still changing.

Why are beaches sandy?

Sand is simply rock that has been broken into very small pieces. These pieces are less than 2 mm (0.08 in) across. Every beach was once made of solid rock. The sea's pounding waves grind coastal rocks into small pieces over thousands of years.

Can plants turn to stone?

The word *petrified* means "turned to stone." This can happen to plants or animals after they have died. Water that has minerals in it dissolves the plant's soft tissue. The harder parts, such as the tubes and bark, don't dissolve. The minerals take less than 100 years to harden. By then, the plant still looks like a plant, but it is now made of stone.

How fast does a glacier move?

Scientists often describe glaciers as being "rivers of ice." Like normal rivers, glaciers flow at different speeds. It depends on the slope of the land, the air temperature, the soil beneath, and many other factors. The fastest, Greenland's Quarayaq glacier, travels up to 24 m (80 feet) a day.

Did a meteorite really kill off the dinosaurs?

Dinosaurs were common across the world for many millions of years. Then all signs of them stopped about 65 million years ago. Their disappearance was a mystery for many years. Most scientists now agree that a large meteorite (a stone from space that crashes to Earth) hit our planet about 65 million years ago. It caused a huge tsunami and sent poisonous gases into the air that killed the dinosaurs.

39

Making a splash

The Earth looks blue when it's viewed from the Moon. That's because two-thirds of its surface is covered with water. Don't be shy – just dive in to find out more about this familiar liquid.

Why do oceans have salt water but rivers have fresh water?

The water in rivers comes from rain. Rainwater does not have any salt in it. The river picks up small amounts of salt from the ground as it travels downhill. This salt enters the ocean at the river mouth. The saltwater mixture becomes saltier as water evaporates.

Are tidal waves and tsunamis the same thing?

No, although many people confuse these two terms. The key is the word *tidal*. Tidal waves are just that – big waves that build up at high tide. A tsunami is a giant wave – or series of waves – caused by an underwater earthquake or volcanic eruption.

TSUNAMI HAZARD ZONE

IN CASE OF EARTHQUAKE GO TO HIGH GROUND OR INLAND

How much does it rain during a monsoon?

An awful lot! A monsoon is a long rainy period. It happens in places where the wind direction changes at the same time each year. India's monsoon develops in late May when the wind shifts to the south. Some areas get more than 65 mm (2.5 in) of rain in twelve hours.

What causes ocean waves?

Wind passing over water creates waves. The water absorbs some of the wind's energy. However, the ocean's enormous water pressure pushes back up. These two opposite pushes create a wave movement that travels across the ocean.

Rain, rain, go away

Everyone likes to talk about the weather – and to moan about it! So, how would you like to be the one who can provide some answers when others ask, "Do you think it's going to rain this weekend – or this century?"

Are rain forests always in hot places?

The most famous rain forests are in the hot tropical regions of South America, Africa, and Asia. But rain forests also develop in cooler parts of the world, as long as those places get enough rain. The Pacific coast of Canada has the largest temperate rain forest.

Where on Earth is the easiest place to forecast the weather?

The British are always talking about the weather – because it's constantly changing. Other parts of the world, though, have much more constant climates. Probably the easiest place to forecast weather is the Atacama Desert in Chile, where no rain fell between 1571 and 1970.

42

Can a butterfly's flapping wing really cause a hurricane?

Maybe! The "butterfly effect" describes how a small change, such as the air movement caused by a butterfly's beating wings, can trigger much bigger changes. It works like a series of dominoes, where the first domino is tiny, and the last one is huge. This effect can make the weather very hard to predict.

Why are there more thunderstorms in the summer?

Thunderstorms need two things to form – moisture and rapidly rising warm air. The late spring and summer are the most common times when these conditions occur. That's because those are the times when the Sun is at its hottest. It warms the air more than at any other time of the year.

Now you've done it

The rest of the planet's animals and plants must sometimes think, "It was OK until you humans came along!" It's true that we have had a huge effect on Earth in the short time we've been here.

Can a polluted lake or river become clean again?

Yes, it can. The first step is to make sure that poisonous chemicals, sewage, and other materials can't flow into the lake. Fresh water needs to flow through to keep it clean. Experts can filter the water to get rid of solids. They can also add tiny organisms to restore the balance of gases dissolved in the water.

When will we run out of oil?

Nobody knows for sure. It is hard to say exactly how much oil is left or exactly how fast the world will use what it does find. Many experts believe that very little oil will be left after 2060. The world will need to find alternative sources of energy before then.

Could a nuclear explosion change the Earth's rotation (spinning)?

Nuclear explosions release more energy than anything else that humans do. Luckily, the energy released by a nuclear explosion is only about one-trillionth of the energy of the Earth's spinning. Scientists compare it to trying to slow the speed of a truck by crashing it into a mosquito.

Do coral reefs only form in tropical waters?

Most coral reefs form in shallow tropical waters. However, scientists are now studying mysterious deep coral reefs, which can form in much colder waters. Coral reefs are under threat from pollution and fishing, so many people are working hard to protect them.

45

Going to extremes

Lots of people get their thrills from taking things to the limit. How would you like to experience what life is like at the extremes of our own planet? Make sure you pack some blankets and fans.

What's in the middle of the Earth?

The middle of the Earth is a ball of metal (nickel and iron). This is the inner core. It's the last layer that you would find if you peeled away the Earth's crust (the top layer), its mantle (sticky melted rock), and its outer core (liquid rock). The inner core is as hot as the Sun's surface – 5,430°C (10,000°F).

How far from the poles can icebergs go before they melt?

Most icebergs remain in the cold Arctic and Antarctic waters. But currents can take them into warmer areas. Icebergs are common off the Atlantic coast of Canada, and some Arctic icebergs drift as far south as Japan before melting.

Why doesn't the half of the Earth facing away from the Sun freeze every night?

We can thank our atmosphere for keeping us warm. The atmosphere stops most of the Sun's heat from radiating (escaping outward). It acts just like a snug blanket to keep us warm. The atmosphere also stops the Earth from getting too hot during the day.

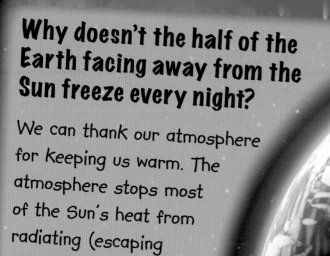

Was the biggest explosion in Earth's history natural or man-made?

The largest man-made explosion was a Russian nuclear weapon exploded in 1961. However, the meteorite that crashed to Earth 65 million years ago and wiped out the dinosaurs made a bigger explosion. It was 1.7 million times more powerful than the Russian weapon.

47

Air we go

Are these facts about the wind, clouds, and air pressure a load of hot air? Of course not! They're all completely true... and they might just blow you away.

Why don't clouds fall down to Earth?

Clouds are made of millions of tiny drops of water and particles of ice. These are so small that they float in the air. Gravity can't pull them to the ground. But these small bits of ice and water can collide and form larger particles or drops. When they do, they fall to the ground as snow or rain.

Ouch, my ears!

Why do our ears pop in planes?

Inside our ears are tiny passages that are filled with air. Normally, this air has the same pressure (outward push) as the air all around us. As we go up in a plane, the air pressure around us gets weaker. But the air inside our ear passages is still the same. The ear has to let air out to change the pressure, and that's what makes our ears pop.

How high up does the atmosphere go?

The atmosphere has five layers. The lowest layer, the troposphere, is where the weather changes. Above it is the stratosphere, where planes travel. Then there's the mesosphere, Earth's shield against meteors. The hot thermosphere is farther out and gives way to the thin exosphere. This outer layer finishes about 6,000 miles (10,000 km) above us.

What makes the wind blow?

Some parts of the atmosphere are warmer than others. Cold air has a higher pressure than warm air (this means it pushes out harder). So cold air always tries to force its way into areas of warmer air. The wind we feel is air doing just that. If there's a big difference in air pressure, then the wind will be strong.

Forcing the issue

Everything on Earth is affected by forces. Whether it's the force of gravity that makes things fall, the magnetic force that guides metal, or the electrical forces that produce lightning, they put on quite a show.

Do planes get struck by lightning?

Passenger planes get hit by lightning about once a year. Luckily, the lightning usually has no bad effect on the plane or passengers. It just leaves a scorch mark where it first hits. The electrical charge travels along the outside of the plane. Most lightning strikes occur when planes are below 3 miles (5 km). Planes usually avoid trouble by flying higher than this.

How do compasses work?

A compass is a magnetic needle that can spin freely. It is attracted by other magnets. The compass works because the Earth itself is like a huge magnet. It has magnetic north and south poles. The painted end of the needle always points north.

Going for the record

These amazing animals are really taking things to the limit! They have the biggest teeth, the most legs... or they're just huge. But would you dare to imagine what it would be like to meet some of these extreme creatures?

Why do centipedes have so many legs?

Centipedes need to be fast because they are hunters. Their legs support their long bodies. They also help centipedes move quickly. A centipede's body is made up of lots of segments that are linked together, a little bit like trains. Each segment has a pair of legs.

What is or was the largest animal ever?

We've all seen pictures of the giant dinosaurs that lived millions of years ago. But the largest-ever animal is still around. The blue whale can grow to 33 m (108 ft) long and weigh 150,000 tons. But this ocean giant eats only tiny krill. Those are tiny shrimplike creatures the size of a jelly bean.

Which animal has the longest teeth?

Maybe you'd get this if the question asked for the longest tooth! That's because the longest single tooth belongs to the narwhal. The narwhal is a type of whale. One of its teeth can grow more than 3 m (10 ft) long. A narwhal uses its long tooth to impress other narwhals and to fight rivals.

нарвал

10

ПОЧТА СССР

1971

Why aren't land animals as **big** as they were in prehistoric times?

The largest dinosaurs lived when the Earth was warmer. It was easier for reptiles (including dinosaurs) to stay warm than it is now. That meant they could be bigger than modern reptiles. After the extinction of the dinosaurs, some mammals grew to a giant size. Human hunters probably caused the extinction of some of those large mammals.

All at sea?

How many times have you heard a story and thought it seemed fishy? Well, all of these stories are fishy... but they're also true!

Do flying fish really fly?

These amazing fish don't really fly like birds. Instead, they're like hang gliders. They glide to escape from attackers. A flying fish builds up speed by wiggling its tail. It then launches from the water and spreads two long fins. These fins are like wings. They allow the fish to glide up to 400 m (1,300 ft) through the air.

Why do sharks have to swim all the time?

Most fish use a swim bladder to float. It's like a balloon. They fill the bladder with gas to float or empty it to sink. Sharks have no swim bladders. They use their fins like a plane's wings to go up or down. That means that they have to keep moving to keep floating!

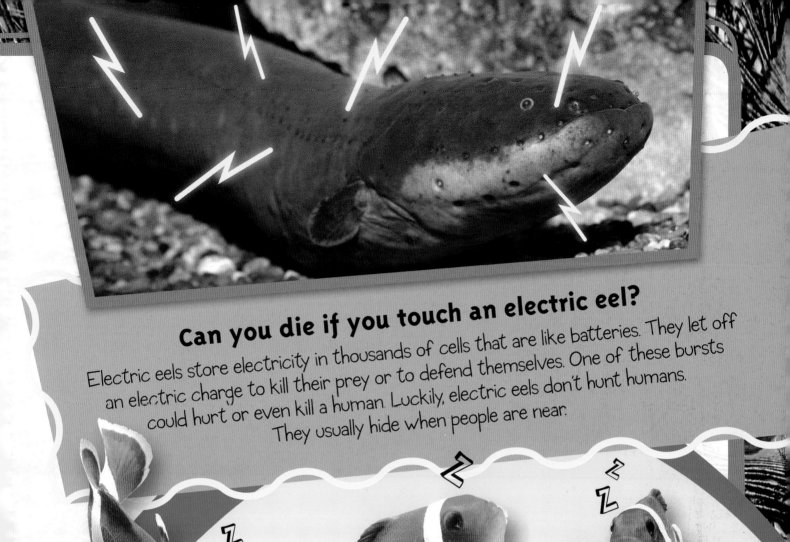

Can you die if you touch an electric eel?

Electric eels store electricity in thousands of cells that are like batteries. They let off an electric charge to kill their prey or to defend themselves. One of these bursts could hurt or even kill a human. Luckily, electric eels don't hunt humans. They usually hide when people are near.

Do fish sleep?

Yes they do, even if it's not like our own sleep. They have no eyelids, so they can't close their eyes. But fish do slow down to rest. Some fish just drift while they rest. Others snuggle into spaces between rocks or underwater plants. Sharks need to swim all the time, so they swim slowly as they rest.

Come to your senses

"I know that forest like the back of my paw." Can you imagine a bear or a dog saying that? You'd find out some pretty strange stuff if animals really could tell you how they find their way around.

Are bats really blind?

Some people think they're blind because they zigzag so much as they fly. But that's not because they can't see straight! It's because they are chasing insects. Bats also use other senses to hunt, including their fantastic sense of hearing.

Which animals have the best eyesight?

The animals with the sharpest eyesight are birds of prey that hunt during the day. Eagles, hawks, and falcons all rely on good eyesight. They need to spot prey as they fly high above the ground. An eagle can spot a hare up to 0.6 miles (1 km) away.

How can whales hear each other across an ocean?

Sound travels faster and longer in water than it does through the air. And low sounds, like whale calls, travel the best. The call of a blue whale is extremely low. It can travel thousands of miles – sometimes even across a whole ocean.

Why do some animals have more than two eyes?

Most large animals have two eyes. Simpler animals such as insects and jellyfish often have many more eyes. These allow them to see in several directions. Jumping spiders have eight eyes, four at the front and four at the back of the head, giving them good all-around vision.

57

Yackety-yak

We humans can communicate in so many ways – text messages, emails, tweets, even old-fashioned talking! Have you ever wondered how animals pass on information to each other?

Do bees really talk to each other by dancing?

Honeybees live together in large hives. Some act like scouts and look for the best flowers to feed on. They return to the hive and do a "waggle dance." The direction of the dance tells others where to find the food.

How do penguin mothers recognize their chicks?

Thousands of penguins live in colonies near Antarctica. Mothers leave their nests to bring back food from the sea. But how do they recognize their own chicks among all the others when they return? They smell them! Penguins can tell the smell of their chicks (and their mates) even among those huge crowds.

Why do wolves howl?

Howling is usually a group effort, even if it starts with one wolf. Wolves live and hunt in packs. Howling is a way of getting the pack excited about going on a hunt – or it could celebrate a successful hunt. It might also be a way of telling other packs to stay away.

Can humans talk to dolphins?

Dolphins "talk" to each other with sounds such as clicks and whistles. Most of these sounds are either too high or too low for humans to hear. But Japanese scientists have produced a machine that might let humans talk to dolphins. It can make – and hear – those high-pitched and low-pitched sounds.

Baby creatures

There's a huge difference in the way animals are born. Some creatures, such as ocean sunfish, lay millions of eggs at a time. Others, such as elephants, give birth to one baby.

Why do kangaroos have pouches?

Kangaroos, like humans, are mammals. They give birth to live young. However, newborn kangaroos are tiny. They are less developed than most newborn mammals. After they are born, they spend another six to eight months in the mother's pouch. Then they are old enough to spend life outside it. Animals with pouches are called marsupials.

Why don't we ever see baby pigeons?

The simplest answer is that their parents spoil them. First of all, most city pigeon nests are hidden on top of buildings or bridges. But more importantly, baby pigeons stay in the nests for a long time. Their parents keep bringing them food. By the time they leave, they look almost like adults.

Can dogs be bred back into wolves?

Yes, they can. Dogs are the descendants of wolves. They sometimes look very different, but they can still have offspring together. The puppy of a wolf and a dog is called a wolfdog. A wolfdog mating with a wolf would produce puppies that were three-quarters wolf.

Do any mammals lay eggs?

Most mammals give birth to live young. But platypuses and four species of anteater – all living in or near Australia – lay eggs. They're still called mammals, though. That's because they have hair and also because the mothers produce milk to feed their young.

What's for dinner?

At school, we learn about having a balanced diet and eating the right things. Most animals, though, must find the right balance between finding food ... and not being eaten themselves!

How do snakes breathe while they swallow their prey?

Snakes can swallow prey that's very wide. They would choke if this food blocked air from getting into their windpipe. But they can stretch the windpipe along the bottom of their mouth. The end of it comes out in front of the food. So the snake can breathe even while it takes its time swallowing.

Can piranhas really strip the flesh off a cow in minutes?

Piranhas are small South American fish with sharp teeth. And yes, a swarm of them really could devour a large animal in minutes. But they usually stick to eating worms, insects, and small fish. And they don't usually swarm to attack. They gang up to defend themselves against attackers.

62

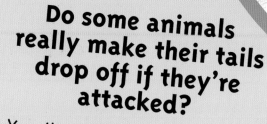

Do some animals really make their tails drop off if they're attacked?

Yes, they do! Some lizards have joins on their tails. They can make their tail drop off if they are in danger from a predator. The tail wiggles around for a few seconds. That's often long enough to fool an attacker into letting them escape. The lizards can grow another tail, but the new tail can't drop off.

Is chocolate poisonous to dogs?

Yes, and they can die from eating too much of it. Chocolate contains theobromine, a chemical that is poisonous to many animals – even humans. But we can break it down and make it harmless. Dogs can't, so the poison builds up inside them. Dark chocolate has lots of theobromine. About 70 g (2.5 oz) could kill a small dog.

Up and away

Have you ever looked up at birds and thought, "I'd love to be able to fly"? Just imagine what it must really be like to take to the air and soar around for hours.

Can birds sleep in midair?

Swifts can spend more than a year in the air. That's from the moment they leave the nest until they return to breed. They have small midair naps. Some people believe that albatrosses must also sleep in midair. These huge seabirds only come to shore to breed. They would be attacked if they slept on the water.

How can birds sit on power lines without being killed?

The birds survive because the electricity in the power lines has no reason to pass through them. A copper wire is easier to pass through than a bird, so the electricity stays in the wire. However, the birds could die if they were touching the wire at the same time as touching something else.

64

What's the largest flock of birds?

The largest recorded flock of birds was in southern Canada in 1866. A flock of passenger pigeons about 1 mile (1.6 km) wide passed overhead. It took 14 hours for the flock to pass by. It was judged to be 300 miles (500 km) long. And the flock contained 3.5 billion birds. Sadly, passenger pigeons became extinct in 1914.

Why are bird droppings white?

What we call "bird poop" is actually mostly urine (pee). Birds use more water from their food and liquids than we do. That means that their urine is nearly dry. Their urine contains a lot of uric acid, which is white.

Fact or fiction?

We've heard so many crazy stories about animals that it's hard to tell which are true and which are legends. Now it's time for you to become a detective and discover the truth.

Do vampire bats really drink blood?

These natives of North and South America do drink blood, but they're not really dangerous. First of all, they're afraid of humans. Second, they don't drink much blood from the cows and horses they land on. They make a shallow bite with their sharp teeth. Then they take about a thimbleful of blood. It's more like a mosquito bite than Dracula.

Did unicorns ever exist?

The unicorn was supposed to be a white horse with a long straight horn jutting out from its head. Ancient people probably saw long-horned antelopes from the side and thought they were unicorns. In late 2012, the mysterious leaders of North Korea said that they had found unicorn skeletons. But scientists still don't believe that the story is true.

Do elephants really go to an "elephants' graveyard" when they're dying?

Legends tell of a place where old elephants go to die. Anyone discovering it would find a huge pile of elephant bones, including tusks that could be sold as ivory. In reality, there's no such place. But there's a little truth behind the legend. Strong African winds sometimes even blow elephant bones into piles.

Do cats really have nine lives?

Cats have only one life, like all living creatures. But this is another legend that is based on a little truth. Cats are able to walk away from falls that would hurt or kill other animals. They have incredible balance and can sometimes fall from skyscrapers without getting hurt. It's not surprising that people think that they have nine lives.

67

It's roundup time

By now you should be able to convince your friends that you're an expert on animal life. If they don't believe you, prove it by rattling off some of these weird and wonderful animal facts.

What do camels store in their humps?

Those lumps are stores of fatty tissue. They're like batteries to give the camel energy and water when it can't eat or drink. Storing fat in lumps is better for a desert animal than having fat covering the whole body. That would make the animal too hot.

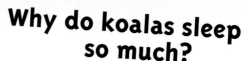

Why do koalas sleep so much?

Koalas don't have a very good diet. They eat only the leaves of eucalyptus trees. And those leaves don't give the koalas much energy. So the koala spends a lot of time asleep. Luckily, it has no predators that could attack it... or disturb its sleep.

How do bats find their way around in the dark?

Bats use a sense called "echolocation" to move around and to find insects to eat. First, they make lots of squeaks. Then their sensitive ears pick up the echoes of the squeaks and can tell exactly where they came from. They use the echoes to build up a picture of the world around them.

Are animals **ticklish?**

Scientists have known for a long time that some animals are definitely ticklish. Our closest relatives – gorillas and monkeys – squirm and laugh like humans. Now it seems that other animals are ticklish, too. A scientist asked a student to tickle a rat as a joke. They were both surprised when the rat wriggled its legs and squeaked – just like laughing.

69

Creepy-crawlies

It's amazing but true: four out of every five animals is an insect. And that's not even including spiders! Spiders don't get to be part of the insect club because they have eight legs, while insects only have six.

Do spiders ever get caught in their own webs?

Only if they're really unlucky. Not every strand of a web is sticky. Moths and other insects don't know which are and which aren't. That's why they get stuck when they fly into the web. But the spider remembers. It stays on the nonsticky strands as it walks across the web.

Why are moths attracted to light?

Moths use the Moon to help guide them at night. Bright lights – such as electric lights or candles – look a lot like the Moon, and this confuses them. As they fly along, they seem to be moving past the Moon, which shouldn't be possible! They keep changing direction to try to fly straight. But instead they fly closer and closer to the light.

Fantastic Forces

Food for thought

Cooking is really just a type of science – except you get to eat the results of your experiments. It's time to put on your white lab coat, or is that an apron?

Why does popcorn **pop**?

A popcorn kernel has an outer case with a starchy inside. There's usually a little water inside, too. When the kernel is heated enough, the water boils. The boiling water becomes a gas and suddenly expands. This "pops" the outer case and turns the kernel inside out. The yummy white fluffy parts are the starch.

How does yeast make bread rise?

Yeast is a type of fungus that becomes active when it is warmed. Bakers mix it into bread dough. Then they leave it somewhere warm. The yeast begins to feed on the sugar in the dough. As it does, it gives off a gas that puffs up the dough.

How can you get words into candy?

British "rock" candy is made by boiling sugar until it looks like white modeling clay. As it cools, it is stretched into long strips. Some parts are dyed and pulled out into long string shapes. The clever part is arranging the dyed strings along the white strips to make words when the whole thing is rolled up. The thick roll is then stretched until it turns into a long piece of rock.

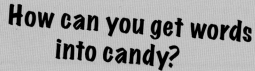

SCIENCE F.A.Q.

F.A.Q. SCIENCE

F.A.Q. SCIENCE

Why do stale cookies get soggy but stale bread goes dry?

Cookies start off dry and have less water than the air around them. Bread and cake have a little more water than the air around them. The water moves from where there's more to where there's less. That means it goes from the air into the cookies – making them soggy. And it goes from the bread into the air – making it drier.

73

It's only natural

Here are a few questions to take you "back to nature." Did you have any idea that there was so much science going on all around you in the natural world?

Why is there often a special smell just before it rains?

The smell is from a gas called ozone. High up in the atmosphere, a layer of ozone protects the Earth from harmful radiation. But the electricity in lightning can produce ozone nearer the ground. The ozone spreads out from rain clouds and often reaches you before the rain arrives.

Why do plants grow better in some soils than in others?

Just like animals, plants need to take in food to grow and stay healthy. Minerals and other natural "plant foods" are called nutrients. Some soils have more nutrients than others, and some soils suit certain plants more than others.

74

Could someone squeeze a piece of coal and turn it into diamond, like Superman?

Superman may have been able to do that trick, but it would never happen in nature. Both coal and diamond are made from a mineral called carbon. But they are very different. Coal started out as plants. Over millions of years, the dead plants were squished into coal. Diamonds formed even longer ago, at very high temperatures deep inside the Earth.

How do solar panels turn sunlight into electricity?

Both sunlight and electricity are made up of tiny objects called particles. The particles in sunlight are called photons. Electricity is a movement of particles called electrons. When photons of sunlight hit the silicon in a solar panel, they knock electrons off the silicon. Those electrons become an electric current.

Changing things

Science is full of things that change from one thing to another, things that change shape, or things that do unusual things. OK, that's enough things! Let's take a look at the science...

What is smoke?

Smoke is all the particles that aren't burned up in a fire. Only water and carbon dioxide are left behind when things are completely burned. But a fire can't burn everything if it doesn't have enough oxygen or if it hasn't become hot enough. So smoke is a mixture of tiny bits of solid, liquid, and gas that are all the leftovers, floating in the air.

What happens when paper is recycled?

Paper is made from wood pulp (wood that's mushed up). The first step of recycling is to add water to the old paper. That makes it easy to mush up and become pulp again. Then the pulp goes through a screen to get rid of ink, glue, and other bits of material. It's then ready to become paper again.

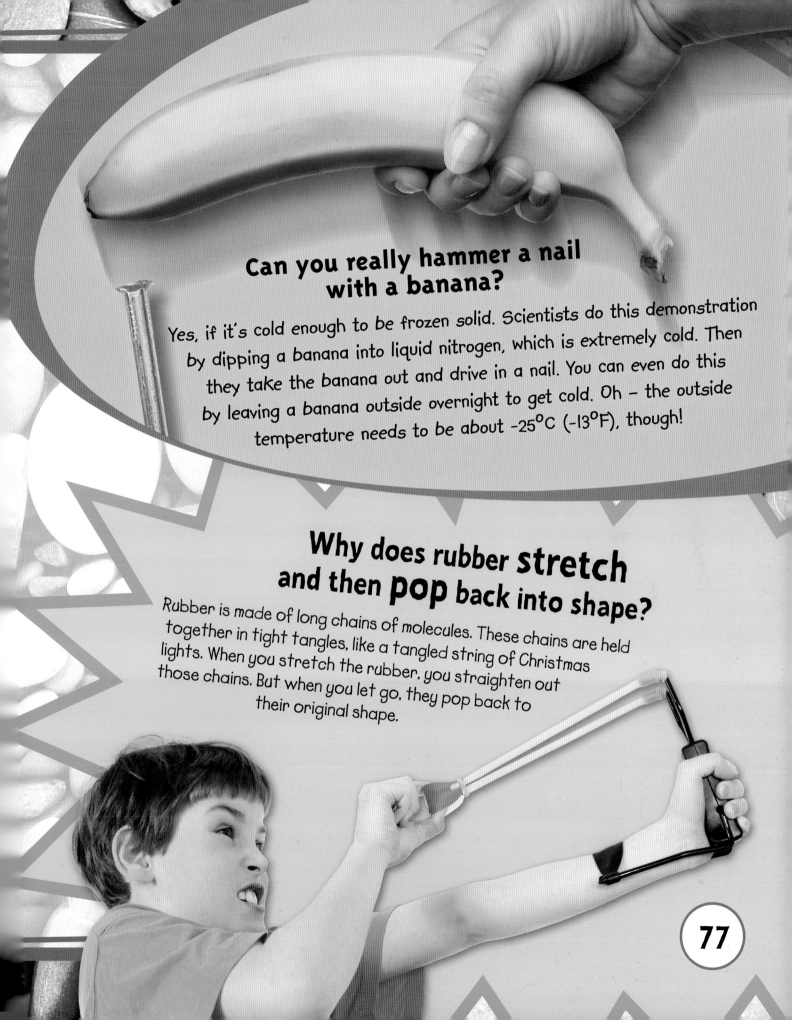

Can you really hammer a nail with a banana?

Yes, if it's cold enough to be frozen solid. Scientists do this demonstration by dipping a banana into liquid nitrogen, which is extremely cold. Then they take the banana out and drive in a nail. You can even do this by leaving a banana outside overnight to get cold. Oh – the outside temperature needs to be about -25°C (-13°F), though!

Why does rubber stretch and then pop back into shape?

Rubber is made of long chains of molecules. These chains are held together in tight tangles, like a tangled string of Christmas lights. When you stretch the rubber, you straighten out those chains. But when you let go, they pop back to their original shape.

77

Whatever floats your boat

Some of the most interesting science facts are all about staying afloat or staying up in the air. It's sink or swim, so hang on in there and check out these answers.

How do huge ships float?

A huge object pushes away lots of water. If it's heavier than the water it pushes away, it will sink. If it's lighter than that water, it will float. A big ship is heavy, but not as heavy as that much water. It has lots of empty spaces that are full of air.

Does all wood float?

Most wood floats because there's lots of air inside it between the wood cells. This makes wood weigh less than water – and float. Some types of wood, such as ebony, are very dense. That means their wood cells are packed so tightly there's not much room for air. These woods will sink in water.

Could you survive if you jumped up just before a falling elevator hit the ground?

It wouldn't work, for two reasons. First, you'd never be able to jump up as fast as the elevator was falling down. Second, even if you could beat the speed of the fall, the elevator would still crash to the bottom. And that would mean the roof of the elevator would crush you as it passed.

How do parachutes work?

These skydivers are being pulled toward Earth by gravity. But an upward force called air resistance is pushing in the opposite direction. The large, flat shape of their parachute increases the amount of air resistance. The parachute is still pulled down by gravity, but because of the push of the air, it falls at a constant, slow speed.

79

Water wonders

Jump in and make a big splash with these questions about the way water behaves. Is water playing tricks on us, or can we get to the bottom of them?

Why do ice cubes float?

It's a good question. Most substances are more dense in their solid form. This means they sink in liquid. But water is unusual. It is less dense in its solid form – ice – than in its liquid form – water. So that's why ice cubes float in water.

How can some insects walk across water?

Water molecules are attracted to each other on all sides. But those on the surface have none above them. This makes them hold on to the ones beside them more strongly. And that hold creates a delicate film which can support light objects without breaking. Scientists call it surface tension.

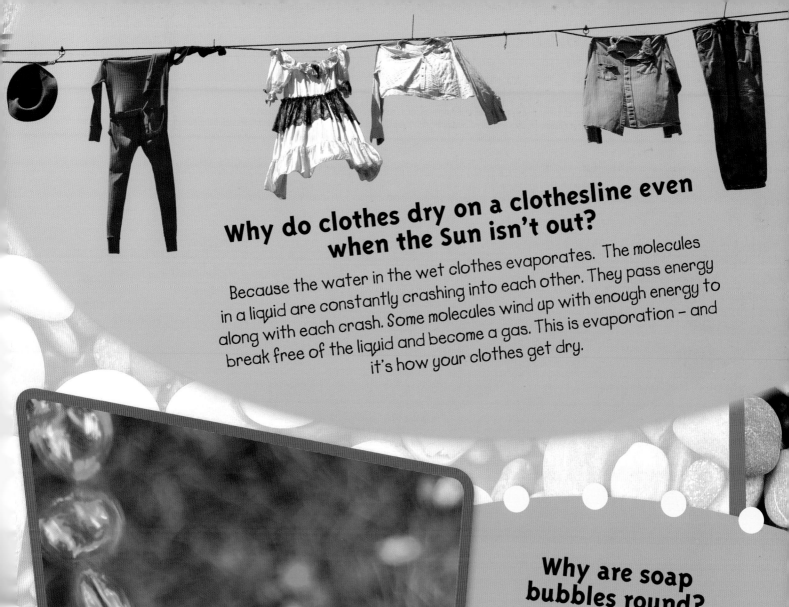

Why do clothes dry on a clothesline even when the Sun isn't out?

Because the water in the wet clothes evaporates. The molecules in a liquid are constantly crashing into each other. They pass energy along with each crash. Some molecules wind up with enough energy to break free of the liquid and become a gas. This is evaporation – and it's how your clothes get dry.

Why are soap bubbles round?

Even if you blow a bubble through a square wand, the bubble is still round. Weird, huh? It happens like this. When you blow through the wand, the bubble forms with air inside. The shape that uses the least energy to form is a sphere (a round shape). So even if it starts off as a long sausage shape while you blow, your bubble will always end up round.

81

Are you stuck?

Here's the crazy place where science becomes magic. Or is it the other way around? It's time to stick together as we find out what sticks, and what doesn't!

How does Velcro work?

Velcro is simple. It has two pieces. One has lots and lots of small plastic hooks. The other piece has loads of tiny loops made of string. The hooks fit into the loops when the pieces go together. Velcro is strong because there are so many locking hooks and loops.

How do nonstick pans work?

Here's an example of chemistry helping you out in everyday life. The inside of the pan is covered in a layer of Teflon. That brand name is easier to say than the official chemical name of this substance – polytetrafluoroethylene. Teflon does not react with other substances, which means that things don't stick to it.

Why do magnets pick up some things and not others?

Magnets can only affect other magnets. What makes something magnetic? Inside any substance, you will find tiny specks of matter called electrons. In a magnetic substance, such as iron, some of those electrons aren't linked to any other electrons and they can line up to form loads of "mini magnets." But in substances that aren't magnetic, all the electrons are linked to each other. They cancel out each other's possible magnetic force.

How does glue make things stick together?

Scientists can't agree on the whole explanation! They know that most glues start off as liquids and finish as solids. To work well, they need to seep into dips and ridges on the things they're attaching. Once they've become solids, the two things are held together. But scientists will have to look more and more closely – down to the tiny level of atoms and beyond – to figure out why the glue really sticks.

Metal workout

Metals are tough and last forever. Right?
What would you think if you found out that
a lot of metals are just softies at heart?

Can stainless steel rust?

Steel is a mixture of iron and carbon. It is strong, but it rusts in much the same way as iron itself. If you add chromium, you produce stainless steel. Chromium gives stainless steel its shine. It also provides a barrier to stop oxygen getting at the steel. Without oxygen, the chemical reaction that produces rust cannot take place.

Why does a coat hanger break if you bend it back and forth?

It's all because of something called metal fatigue. Fatigue means "tiredness," and that's a good description of what happens. Bending the metal back and forth opens up tiny cracks in the surface of the metal. The cracks get wider and wider until... the hanger breaks.

Why does oil make tools last longer?

The metal parts of tools look smooth, but their edges are uneven. When they move against each other, these uneven parts catch. The tool doesn't work so well, and the moving parts wear down. Oil keeps those parts from touching each other. They can still move back and forth, but they don't catch anymore.

Why does a razor blade get blunt if it only has to cut hair?

You'd have to look closely – really closely – at the blade to find out. A human hair is harder to cut than copper wire of the same size. It knocks atoms off the edge of the blade when the razor hits it. Lots of hairs knock lots of atoms off. And without the straight line of atoms forming an edge, the blade gets dull and blunt.

Read all about it

You don't need to be reading a textbook to learn about science. Just take a closer look at the paper, ink and pencils that you use every day.

Why does old paper turn yellow?

Paper is made of wood. The part of wood called cellulose makes paper white. But wood also contains a dark substance called lignin. This adds strength to wood. In time, the lignin in paper breaks down and forms yellow acids. And it's these that turn the paper yellow.

Can you stick two books together without using glue?

Yes, and the secret comes from the force of friction. Face the open pages of two paperback books toward each other. Slowly fan the pages, so that the pages of each book extend about 5 cm (2 in) into the other. Now try to pull them apart. It's hard because the force of friction builds up with each overlap.

Potty Plants

It's a jungle out there!

Almost everywhere you look, you see plants – sometimes so many that it would be impossible to count them all. But just how much do you know about all of these green inhabitants of planet Earth?

Are tomatoes fruits or vegetables?

Even some scientists disagree about this. The simple answer is that tomatoes are fruits. Why? Because scientists define a fruit as the mature ovary of a plant, containing seeds. All the other parts of a plant – such as leaves (e.g. lettuce), stems (e.g. celery), and roots (e.g. carrots) are called vegetables.

Can you eat flowers?

You certainly can! In fact, you may have eaten some this week if you've had broccoli or cauliflower. These are the flowering parts of plants. Many attractive flowers, such as violets and roses, can also be eaten or used to make teas. But it's important to remember that some flowers are poisonous, and we should never simply assume that a flower is edible.

Are peanuts really nuts?

No. Peanuts are the seeds of legumes – members of a plant family that includes beans. Legume fruits form hard shells known as pods, which contain two or more seeds. Peas – which everyone knows grow in pods – are also legumes. Almonds and walnuts are true nuts. They are one-seeded fruit of full-sized trees and grow inside a hard shell.

Why is grass green not blue?

Grass uses light from the Sun to create the energy it needs to survive and grow. This energy-producing process is called photosynthesis. It relies on a chemical found in plants called chlorophyll, which is green!

Try this for size

Plants can range in size from tiny speck-like seeds to towering giant redwoods. And the more you find out about them, the more they will grow on you!

Is it really possible to drive a car through a tree?

Yes. In the giant redwood and sequoia forests of northern California, there are several trees that have been hollowed out so that cars can drive through them. One of the most famous is 96 m (315 ft) tall. A road passes through a hole in the trunk that is 1.83 m (6 ft) wide and 2.06 m (6 ft 9 in) high.

What is the largest fruit in the world?

The jackfruit tree produces a fruit that weighs more than a ten-year-old child. It grows in the rain forests of India and Southeast Asia. The fruits can be 90 cm (36 in) long, 47 cm (19 in) wide, and can weigh 36 kg (80 lb). They taste like banana, but more sour.

Which plant has the largest seeds?

The world's largest seed comes from the Coco de Mer. This is a type of palm tree that is native to islands in the Indian Ocean. Its seeds form inside giant egg-shaped fruit. These can weigh more than 17 kg (37 lb).

Can corn really grow "as high as an elephant's eye"?

This is a line from a famous American song – but is it just a tall tale? Most elephants' eyes are about 3 m (10 ft) off the ground, and most corn is harvested when it is about 2.5 m (8 ft) tall. But with enough rain, sunshine, and fertilizer, corn can grow up to 4 m (13 ft) or even higher. So in fact, corn can grow even taller than an elephant's eye!

91

Jobs to do

Imagine a sergeant barking out these orders: "Flowers – attract some insects. Roots – we need more water. Thorns – keep those deer away!" Each part of a plant really does have a job to do, even if no one's there to order it around.

Why do some trees have needles instead of leaves?

The needles of evergreen trees are really leaves. Like other leaves, they contain chlorophyll, the green chemical that helps plants make their own food. Evergreens grow where it is either dry or cold. Their narrow, hard needles lose less water from evaporation than normal leaves. Their long, thin shape also protects them from the extreme cold.

What's the "point" of thorns?

Plants have no way of escaping from hungry animals looking for tasty leaves or blossoms for their next meal. That's why some plants, such as roses and cacti, grow thorns to protect themselves. A deer might think twice about sticking its delicate nose through a bunch of thorns just to reach a tasty rosebud.

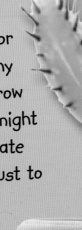

Do a tree's roots grow as deep downward as the tree grows upward?

Most tree roots are surprisingly shallow. Even some of the tallest trees have roots that go down less than 45 cm (18 inches). Trees can be blown over in strong winds because they don't have deep roots to anchor them. Although the roots are shallow, they can be wide. Some root networks are three times as wide as the branches above.

Why do trees have bark?

Trees and shrubs actually have two layers of bark. The inner layer is made up of long, tubelike cells called xylem. They transport water and minerals up from the roots. The outer layer is made up of dead cells. These cells have hardened to form a protective barrier against insects. They also stop water from the inner bark evaporating.

93

Peculiar plants

Do you think that plants just sit there and don't do much? You'll know better once you get to know these weirdos. You might want to stand back or even hold your nose!

Do Mexican jumping beans really jump?

Yes, they really do bounce, but they're not really beans, and it's not the plant that's doing the jumping. The larva of a small moth eats into the seed casing of a Mexican shrub. Protected from the desert sun, it grows into an adult moth. But if it feels too warm inside, it swings to try and move into the shade. And that makes the "bean" seem to jump.

Why do nettles sting?

Nettles sting for the same reason that some plants have thorns: to protect themselves. Nettle flowers are protected from plant-eating mammals by the stinging leaves all around them. However, insects are still able to land on the flowers and carry away their pollen, so that the nettles can reproduce.

What is the smelliest fruit?

The durian grows in Southeast Asia and looks a little bit like a large, thorny pineapple. But its smell is what makes the durian famous. It's been described as a cross between rotten onions and dirty gym socks! Some people actually like the smell and describe the durian as the "king of fruits."

Why do some cacti only bloom for one day a year?

The Purple Ball Cactus needs to attract insects to its flowers in order to reproduce. However, a delicate bloom like a rose or tulip would shrivel in the desert heat. The cactus solves this problem by making a flower with a protective waxy covering. However, it takes a lot of effort to make this flower... so much that it only blooms for one day a year!

95

Changing nature

Plants were around for millions of years before the first humans showed up. But ever since we've discovered them, we've been changing them: their shape, their size, and even their genes.

Which plants did the first human farmers grow?

Scientists are looking for evidence of when humans first began farming. In 2006, scientists uncovered a collection of figs and humans remains in Israel that were 11,300 years old. The figs were a type that needed to be planted – not just picked. Another recent find, in Korea, suggests that farmers might have been growing rice 15,000 years ago.

Why are bonsai trees so small?

Bonsai is the Japanese art of producing small trees and shrubs to look like fully grown trees. Their owners trim and prune small branches to make them grow in this unusual way. Most bonsai ("tray-planted") trees are only about 50 cm (20 in) tall.

Why are carrots orange?

Until the late 1600s, carrots could be purple, white, red, or yellow. According to one theory, today's orange carrots are descendants of the "Long Orange Dutch Carrot," which was first described in 1721. This was created by Dutch farmers who were looking for a way to commemorate their leader William of Orange. They crossbred different carrot varieties until they found a hardy orange variety.

What are GM crops?

Some scientists are working to alter the genes in plants to make them more productive or better able to resist pests. Plants that have been modified (changed) like this are called genetically modified (GM) crops. But there's a big debate about the effects of GM crops on the environment.

Going to extremes

We humans can survive in baking deserts or freezing polar regions, and we have even flown to the Moon. Plants can live in some extreme places, too...

Can plants grow at the North or South Poles?

No plants can grow at the North or South Poles because the temperatures are so cold all year. A few plants manage to survive in the Arctic region near the North Pole and the Antarctic region near the South Pole. These tend to be simple plants such as moss or tough grasses.

Does a cactus have any leaves?

Its leaves, called spines, look like sharp needles. A leaf shaped like an oak or beech leaf would shrivel up in the hot desert sun. The spines protect the cactus against plant-eating animals.

Why are there no trees on Mount Everest and other high mountains?

The air temperature goes down the higher up you climb. The temperature on the highest mountains is around -40° C (-40° F). High winds, even on lower mountains, blow soil away so that only rock remains. These conditions are no good for plants.

Do plants grow on any other planets?

So far, scientists have found no evidence of any type of life on other planets. Most are either too hot or too cold. NASA scientists have sent a robot vehicle called Curiosity to study Mars. It might find evidence that plants did grow there long ago, when the planet's atmosphere was more like ours.

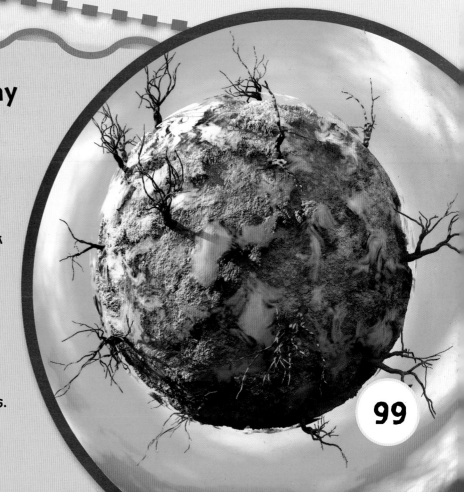

99

Eat your greens!

Plants have a starring role whenever it's time for us to eat – from the tastiest chocolate to the slimiest serving of spinach on your dinner plate.

Does spinach really make you **strong?**

For years, people believed that spinach made you strong because it contains a lot of iron (which strengthens muscles). In reality, spinach has no more iron than most other green vegetables. It is still good for you, though. The vitamins it contains protect the heart, bones, and eyes.

Are green potatoes really poisonous?

Green potatoes contain a poison called solanine, which makes you feel sick and gives you bad headaches. Potatoes make solanine when they are exposed to warmth and light. Warmth and light also lead the potato to produce chlorophyll. So it's the green chlorophyll that's the clue that there is poison in the potato.

Could a plant grow in your stomach if you swallowed a seed?

Luckily, this is not a problem. Think about what plants need to survive – water, carbon dioxide, light, and nutrients from soil. Of these, only water could be available in your stomach, and even then, it would be mixed with strong acid. So the conditions just aren't right for growing plants in your stomach.

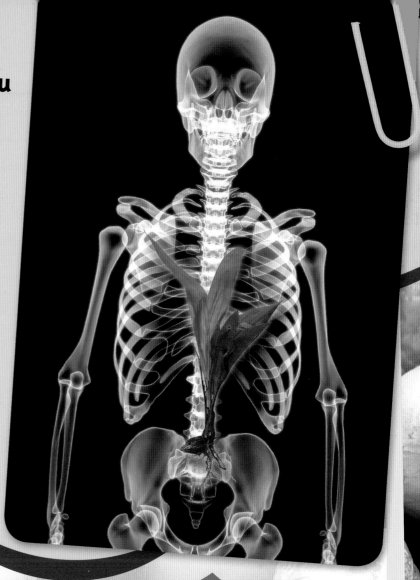

Where does chocolate come from?

Chocolate comes from the beans (or "seeds") of the cacao tree. These beans are left in pots to ferment and become less bitter. Then they are roasted and their outer shells are removed. What's left, the "nibs," are crushed into a paste. Chocolate makers then mix in sugar, vanilla, and often milk. The paste is mashed for days and then heated several times. The result is delicious chocolate.

Don't get soaked!

Every plant needs water to survive, but that usually means taking it in – not living in it. Here are some plants that really make a splash.

Can you really sit on a lily pad?

You can't sit on just any water lily, but some tropical species are large enough to hold a young child. The giant water lily of the Amazon region produces more than 40 leaves, which rest on the calm water surface. The leaves grow up to 2.5 m (8 ft) across and can support up to 45 kg (100 lb) without sinking.

Is seaweed a plant?

The answer is "almost." Seaweed is a type of algae. Like plants, it can create its own food using photosynthesis. Unlike plants, seaweed has no roots or tubes running through it to deliver food and water. That's because every part of it is touching water and able to make food, so there's no need for a system of "pipes."

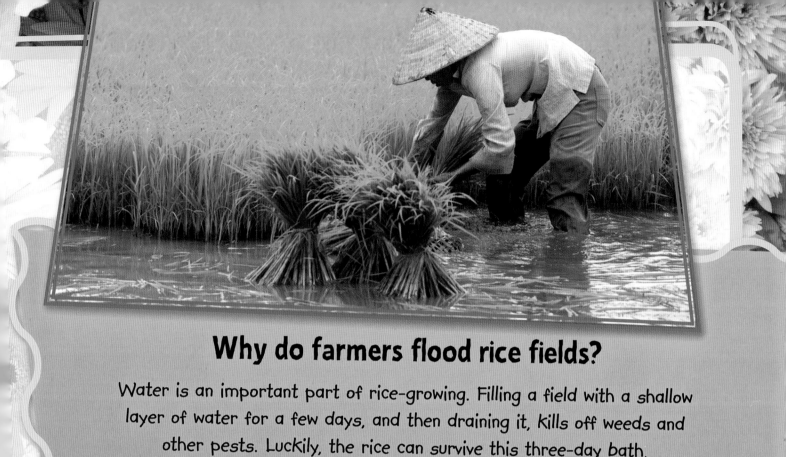

Why do farmers flood rice fields?

Water is an important part of rice-growing. Filling a field with a shallow layer of water for a few days, and then draining it, kills off weeds and other pests. Luckily, the rice can survive this three-day bath, so it continues to grow.

Why does a plant die if you overwater it?

All plants need some water to survive and grow, but they will die if they have too much. This is because plant roots need to be able to absorb gases from the air. They do not work properly if they are underwater because they can't send water and nutrients to the rest of the plant. More houseplants die from overwatering than from lack of water.

Just wondering

Do you feel like a plant expert yet? Here are two final questions and answers to kick-start your investigations into the amazing world of trees, shrubs, flowers, and seeds...

What is the world's most poisonous plant?

Most plant experts agree that the castor-oil plant is the deadliest. Its poison, called ricin, is contained in the seeds. Swallowing as few as four of these beans leads to a painful death in about five days unless the person is treated by a doctor.

Are mushrooms plants?

They grow on the ground. People eat them. Mushrooms must be plants, right? The answer is no! Mushrooms lack one of the most important features of plants – the ability to make their own food. Instead, mushrooms feed on dead and decaying plants, which is why we see them on old tree stumps.

Sunny side up

You've seen loads of sunrises and beautiful sunsets, but how much do you really know about the Sun? It's time to learn some more about your local star.

What is the Sun made of?

The Sun is a giant ball of gas. About 70 % of the gas is hydrogen. Most of the rest is the gas helium. The Sun has an incredibly hot core. That's where it burns hydrogen into helium. The burning releases huge amounts of energy.

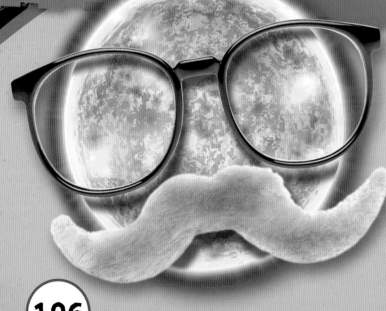

How old is the Sun?

The Sun was "born" 4.6 billion years ago. It formed from a spinning ball of gas and dust. This huge ball began to spin faster and faster as it got smaller. Scientists believe that it will continue to shine for another 5 billion years. That's quite a sunny forecast!

Why does the Sun have **spots**?

Sunspots are parts of giant magnets inside the Sun. Our Sun has a magnetic field, but it gets twisted because the Sun spins so fast. Parts of this magnetic field pop out of the surface of the Sun and we see them as spots. They seem dark, but that's only because they give off a little less light than the rest of the Sun.

How much energy does the Sun produce?

A family car produces about 200 horsepower. The amount of energy that the Sun produces in one second is 500,000,000,000,000,000,000,000 horsepower. That's enough to melt an ice bridge that's 2 miles (3 km) wide, 1 mile (1.6 km) thick, and goes all the way from the Earth to the Sun – in one second!

Close companions

Earth is just one of the eight planets that move around the Sun. Together they're known as the Solar System. But just how much are the other planets like ours?

How did Saturn get its rings?

Those rings aren't solid like hula hoops. They're made up of many, many tiny solid objects floating around Saturn. The rings formed when the planet pulled larger objects, such as comets or even moons, toward it. Those objects crashed into each other and broke up. And the pieces are what we see as rings.

Which planets have the longest – and shortest – days?

A day is one complete turn on a planet's axis. Venus has the longest day. A "Venus day" lasts 243 "Earth days." It's even 18 "Earth days" longer than a "Venus year"! Jupiter has the shortest day. A day on Jupiter lasts just under ten hours.

Why isn't Pluto a planet anymore?

People began to wonder whether Pluto really was a planet in the late 1990s. For one thing, it turned out to be much smaller than they had thought. Astronomers (space scientists) gathered in 2005 to decide. They said that Pluto was almost a planet – but not quite. And that's because it hasn't cleared its orbit around the Sun of other objects, the way real planets do.

Could there be a planet just like Earth that's always hidden on the far side of the Sun?

People have wondered about that for many hundreds of years, but it's not the case. We can tell because of gravity. This force means that everything in space pulls on everything else. Scientists can notice that pull even if it is weak. Another planet like Earth would pull on Mercury and Venus. But no one has ever noticed any such effect.

Over the moon

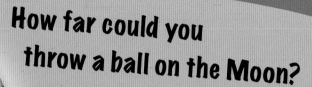

We've all gazed with wonder at the full moon. But imagine how it would be to have five or six or even ten moons passing overhead each night. That's what it's like on some planets.

How far could you throw a ball on the Moon?

The Moon's gravity is six times weaker than Earth's. That means that moving objects can go six times farther. Also, the Moon has no air to slow moving objects as air does on Earth. So if you can throw a ball 30 m (100 ft) here, then on the Moon, it would go 200 m (660 ft) or more.

Is it windy on the Moon?

There's no wind on the Moon at all. That's because you need an atmosphere to create wind. It's all about gases warming up and cooling in different places. American astronauts put a U.S. flag on the Moon when they arrived in 1969. The flag was wrinkled inside a strong frame. That made it look like a flag blowing in the wind.

110

Do other planets have moons?

Yes. The only planets that don't have moons are the two closest to the Sun – Mercury and Venus. Mars has two moons, and scientists are constantly finding smaller moons around the outer planets. Jupiter and Saturn each have more than a dozen.

How does the Moon cause tides?

The Moon pulls on the Earth with the force of gravity. The part of Earth that's closest to the Moon gets pulled a little closer. That closest part is often the sea. We see the water rise as it's pulled slightly to the Moon. When the Moon pulls the sea closer, it's high tide. When the Earth turns and the sea is facing away from the Moon, it's low tide.

Up, up, and away

What goes up must come down. At least, that's what we expect here on Earth. Is it any different if we travel into space? It's time to find out.

What's the farthest that anything from Earth has gone?

The United States launched the uncrewed *Voyager 1* spacecraft in 1977. Its mission was to send back information about planets in our solar system. Since then, it has sped farther and farther away from Earth. Scientists believe that it left our solar system in 2012. It is now nearly 11.2 billion miles (18 billion km) from Earth.

How much junk have humans left in space?

Bits of rockets fall back to Earth whenever something is launched into space. Some debris falls off spacecraft that are orbiting Earth and it usually stays in orbit. At least 5,000 tons of this "space junk" is circling the Earth right now.

How long would it take to fly to Mars?

A return trip to Mars would take more than a year. It would last about 420 days. That's a long time to be stuck in a spacecraft. The missions to the Moon about 40 years ago only lasted about a week each.

Could a plane travel into space if it had enough fuel?

The fuel wouldn't be the real problem. A plane wouldn't be able to fly fast enough to escape Earth's gravity. The nearest thing to a plane in space were NASA's space shuttles. They could come back to Earth and land at an airport. But they needed to get a piggyback ride on a rocket to get into space in the first place.

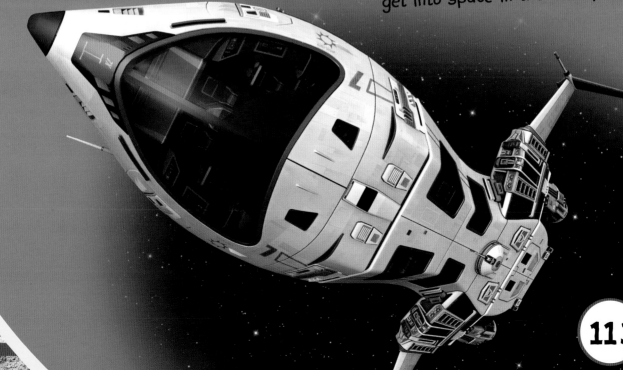

Here comes trouble

You've probably had to mop or sweep up after you've spilled or broken something. Would things be worse if you'd made that mistake in space – or on the Moon?

DO NOT OPEN!

Why is it a bad idea to open the door on a spacecraft?

The air inside the spacecraft has pressure (an outward push), just like air on Earth. But outside the spacecraft, there's no pressure. So the air would be pushed out into space if you opened the door. You'd get pushed out with it. Also, you'd have no air to breathe outside the spacecraft.

Which would fall faster on the Moon: a hammer or a feather?

There would be no difference. That doesn't happen on Earth because of the air. It holds some things up, such as feathers and parachutes. Other things fall quickly. On the Moon, there's no air to slow down a fall. Astronaut Buzz Aldrin took a feather and a hammer to the Moon. He dropped them – and they landed at the same time!

Could we protect Earth if an asteroid were coming straight at us?

Scientists believe that we could send a rocket to blow it up with a powerful weapon. But we would have to act quickly. The blast would blow the asteroid into thousands of pieces. These pieces could still be dangerous if the explosion was close to Earth.

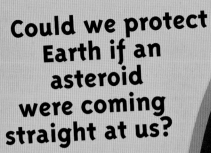

What would happen if you spilled water in space?

If you were inside a spacecraft, water would float in balls. Air would be pressing in on it from all sides and holding it together. But if you were outside the ship, there would be no air pressure. The water would turn into a gas and spread apart completely.

115

Sky-high science

People have been trying to make sense of the sky above us since the earliest times. Modern tools make that search even more exciting. Let's take off on a journey of discovery.

Can scientists really listen to signals from distant stars?

Yes. When we look at stars with our naked eye or through a telescope, we are looking at light. That's a form of radiation that we can see. But stars give out lots more radiation than just visible light. They also send out radio waves. Scientists use what look like huge satellite dishes to pick up those waves. They turn the radio signals into sounds, so that they can listen to them.

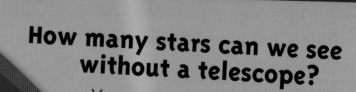

How many stars can we see without a telescope?

You can see about 2,000 stars on a dark night with no Moon in the sky. You also need to be far away from city lights. Any bright light makes it harder to see faint objects such as stars in the sky.

Are astronomy and astrology the same thing?

No. Astronomy is the science related to things in the sky. Astronomers study the Sun, Moon, planets, stars – everything that's in the universe. Astrology is a belief that the stars and planets affect how people behave.

JANUARY FEBRUARY MARCH APRIL MAY JUNE JULY AUGUST SEPTEMBER OCTOBER NOVEMBER DECEMBER

What is a light year?

Quick answer – it doesn't measure time. It's a way of making it easier to understand the vast distances in space. Light travels about 186,000 miles (300,000 km) in a second. A light year is the distance that light travels in a year – around 5.88 trillion miles (9.5 trillion km).

117

Tighten your space helmet

You've squeezed yourself into your spacesuit, and you're ready for takeoff. But how will you feel once the excitement wears off? Will you be the same person after a year inside that spacecraft? And is that a line for the bathroom?

How do astronauts go to the bathroom?

Their toilets look normal, but they have one big difference. Toilets on Earth use gravity to make liquids and solids land in the water. That water gets flushed away. In space, all of it would float and make a bad mess. So space toilets use air to suck liquids and solids away.

ASTRONAUTS

Who was the last person to walk on the Moon?

U.S. astronaut Eugene Cernan flew to the Moon twice. The second time was in December 1972. That was the last mission to the Moon. Cernan was the last man to get into the spacecraft heading back to Earth. He was also the last person to *drive* on the Moon. Part of his job was to drive a Moon buggy.

What is the longest anyone has ever been in space?

Valeri Polyakov spent 438 days in Russia's Mir space station in 1994–5. He broke the previous record by 74 days. Polyakov spent a long time in space to find out whether astronauts could manage a trip to Mars. Most people think that such a mission would be at least as long as Polyakov's time in space.

Do astronauts grow taller in space?

They do, because they are weightless in space. Everyone's backbone is slightly curved here on Earth. That's because of gravity pulling on us. Without that gravity, astronauts' backbones straighten out. They can gain about 5 cm (2 in) by the end of their flight.

Heavens above

The night sky is much more than just a pretty background painting. It is our window to the whole universe! Remember that next time you look up on a clear night.

Why is the North Star so important?

Our spinning Earth means that the stars seem to go around in circles. We're the ones spinning, but they seem to move – except for one. The North Star is above our North Pole. Everything seems to spin around it. Sailors could always find north if they spotted that star. This allowed them to figure out their direction.

Who gets to go on the International Space Station?

This permanent space lab has been orbiting the Earth since 1998. Five space organizations have teamed up to work on it – the United States, Russia, Europe, Japan, and Canada. Each of these chooses astronauts. The organizations then meet to decide which repairs or scientific tests they need to do. Then they choose the best astronauts to match the jobs.

Did cavemen see the same constellations as us?

Yes, they saw the stars in almost exactly the same places. The patterns of constellations have looked much the same for millions of years. The stars that make them up are speeding along different paths. But to us, they hardly seem to move because they're so far away.

GANYMEDE

EUROPA

CALISTO

IO

Can we see any of the moons of other planets?

Big telescopes can see dozens of moons near other planets. But even with binoculars or a small telescope, you can see four other moons. They all belong to the planet Jupiter and they are the first moons of another planet that anyone ever noticed. The famous Italian scientist Galileo Galilei discovered them with a homemade telescope in 1610.

121

Long ago and far away ...

When you think about the size and age of the universe, it can make you feel very small! It's hard to make sense of such large numbers.

Just what happened in the Big Bang?

Most astronomers think that the universe began in a sudden expansion (a rush of growth) that lasted much less than a second. This Big Bang happened about 14 billion years ago. It made everything that we know – matter, energy, and even time itself. The universe then cooled, and all the stars and planets formed.

How close is the nearest star, other than the Sun?

The next closest star is called Proxima Centauri. It is about 4.3 light years away. That doesn't sound so far. But that same distance works out as 25,300 billion miles (39,900 billion km).

How do planets form?

A huge spinning ball of gas turns into a star. Then pieces of that giant ball break off and form smaller balls. Those balls become planets. They continue to move in the same direction as when they broke off. But by then, they're spinning around the star in their own orbits.

What is the most distant object that we can see without a telescope?

That far-off object is the Andromeda galaxy. It contains billions and billions of stars, but we see it as a faint cloud. It's about 13 million trillion miles (21 million trillion km) away.

123

That's life!

Are we the only living things in the whole universe? People have wondered that since they first looked at the stars. But maybe we now have the tools to find out!

Why do people think that aliens are green?

It all began about sixty years ago. Newspapers began printing stories about people seeing aliens in "flying saucers." Several witnesses said that the flying saucers were full of "little green men." That idea stuck because it was strange and interesting.

Has anyone found life on another planet?

Not yet, but we keep trying. The best chances in our Solar System are on Mars and on some of the moons of Jupiter and Saturn. Scientists are looking for traces of even the most basic life. At the same time other scientists are searching for signs of intelligent life anywhere in the universe.

Greetings from Mars!

Did scientists find signs of life on a meteorite from Mars?

In 1984, scientists found an unusual meteorite. It had begun its long journey on Mars about 16 million years ago. It seemed that something living might have made some tiny holes inside the meteorite. Some scientists remain hopeful. Others say that the holes aren't proof of life because they're too small.

Is there really a message for other forms of life on a spacecraft sent from Earth?

The United States launched the *Pioneer* spacecraft in 1972. The outside of it has a message for any intelligent creatures that might find it in some far-off part of space. Pictures show maps of our Solar System, human beings and *Pioneer*'s route through space.

It's out of this world

You've been out of this world and back again quite a few times in this book. And you're ready to begin exploring space on your own now. Here is some helpful information to guide you on that wonderful voyage.

What are the asteroids' names?

Many thousands of asteroids are in a band between Mars and Jupiter. The largest and brightest have names. Some are named after Greek or Roman gods, such as Ceres. Other names, such as Pasachoff, commemorate scientists. Most asteroids just go by codes, such as C2231.

What is a blue moon?

The Moon orbits around the Earth in just under 28 days. That's the time it takes to go from one full moon to the next. But eleven of our months are longer than that. That means that the date of the full moon gets earlier each month. We call it a blue moon when one month has two full moons. It doesn't happen often — only "once in a blue moon."

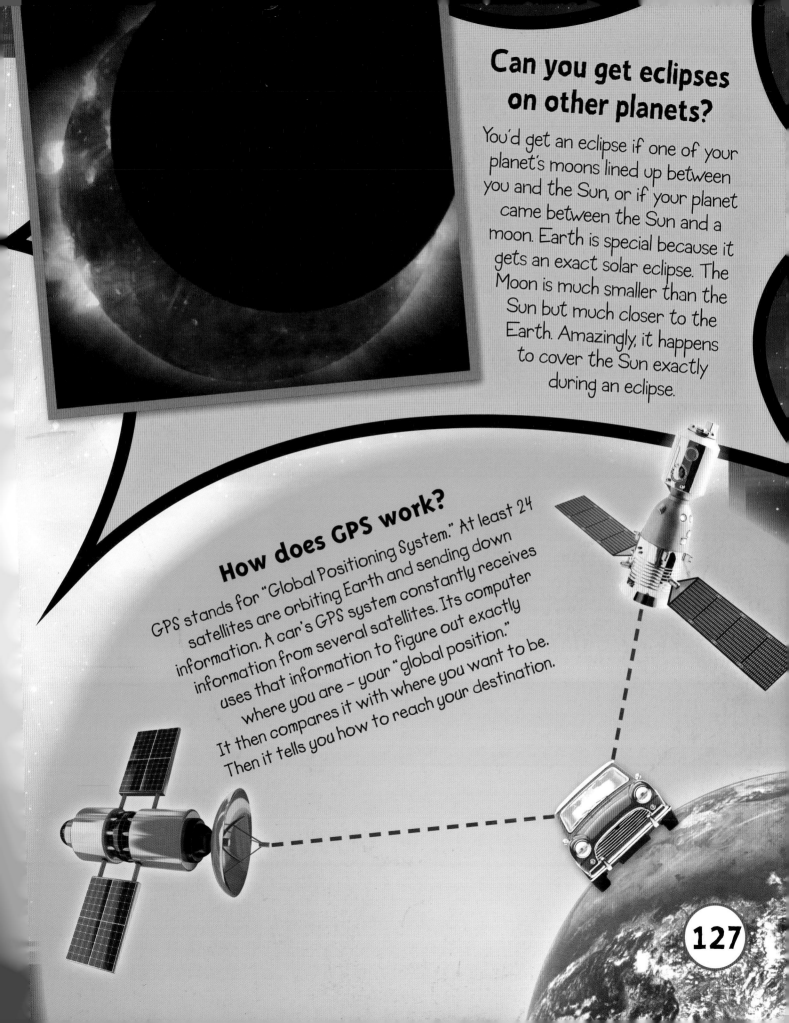

Can you get eclipses on other planets?

You'd get an eclipse if one of your planet's moons lined up between you and the Sun, or if your planet came between the Sun and a moon. Earth is special because it gets an exact solar eclipse. The Moon is much smaller than the Sun but much closer to the Earth. Amazingly, it happens to cover the Sun exactly during an eclipse.

How does GPS work?

GPS stands for "Global Positioning System." At least 24 satellites are orbiting Earth and sending down information. A car's GPS system constantly receives information from several satellites. Its computer uses that information to figure out exactly where you are – your "global position." It then compares it with where you want to be. Then it tells you how to reach your destination.

Hey, lighten up!

Nothing moves faster than light. But the light from far-off stars still takes many years to reach us. It's time to shed some light on light – and why it means so much in our universe.

Why are **black holes** black?

Black holes form when lots of material gets squashed together. That can happen when a star collapses. Lots of material in a small space means that the force of gravity gets really strong. It's so strong that nothing can escape – not even light! And when we can't see light, an object looks black.

Why do stars twinkle?

They're not really twinkling. If you watched them from space, they would seem like steady dots of light. But we're looking at them through the gases in our atmosphere. Changing winds and heat can also change the way light seems to come through the atmosphere. The light might seem brighter for a split second, or darker. And that's what looks like twinkling.